HOW TO GET A MAN

AND KEEP A MAN

ARIANE ROBINSON

Copyright

How To Get A Man And Keep A Man/Ariane Robinson

© 2019, Ariane Robinson/AR Publishing's

ISBN (978-0-578-59264-0)

Cover Art By: Cover_Designa1

Book Edited By: Mike Valentino

Photography By: Transcending Memories Photography

Table of Contents

Introduction

I bet you're wondering what makes me qualified to give such advice and what makes me the relationship expert? Well, let me tell you a little about myself. I'll start off by saying I've been in one relationship my entire life since I began dating. I met my husband when I was a teenager. We've been together for 15 years, married, going on 10 years. Throughout that time, I've witnessed numerous friends, associates and family members have less than successful relationships. Not only have I observed this, I have been able to coach them and help them with my own valid tips that I use in my own relationship, to get men and to rehabilitate their relationships. After so many years and so many families, I've helped I kept hearing, "you need to write a book, you need to share your expertise." Well, after hearing that so many times, I decided that it was time for me to help as many women as possible with my advice and my expert tips experienced throughout my lifetime. And that's what makes me an expert.

<u>CHAPTER ONE</u>

Welcome to How to Get a Man, and more importantly, how to Keep a Man, the book. After reading this book, you will have a better understanding of what to do and what not to do to get and to keep a man.

In my opinion, men are like dogs. Just like any dog trained or not, they're going to try you to see what they can get away with. If you have your dumpster open and you have an unleashed dog or a dog on a long leash, they're going to get into that dumpster. But if there's a short leash, then they can't, and I think men need to be controlled or trained in the same way you would do a dog.

Men are physically stronger than women, but when it comes to the mental part, that's where you'll find a man's weakness. They think that because they're men, they're naturally superior, but in reality they are not. So, when it's time to pass on things like temptations, they don't do it nonetheless, because they don't look at that as a weakness but as simply a part of "being a man."

Men have a hard time being committed and faithful to one woman because, amongst other reasons, society portrays cheating by a man as natural and therefore okay. Like I said, men are dogs. That's as it's always been. So, you just don't expect good behavior to occur naturally or automatically. And most men give into temptation, first and foremost because they feel like they're men, and that's what, at least subconsciously, is expected of them. And it's acceptable.

At the same time, a woman's strongest attribute is her mind. We, for the most part, overcome any obstacle. Give us a problem, we most definitley will figure it out. While it's not always that easy for a man.

I cannot stress this enough, men are like children and should be treated the same way you would treat a young boy. A young boy needs to be taught how to properly interact and conduct themselves. Men like to act like their feelings don't get hurt, just like young boys. However, the truth is, their feelings do get hurt, they're just not that great at articulating themselves and their feelings.

Women are goddesses. You see, we like to be worshiped. We already know our own strengths and how strong we are independently. However, we want to a man to acknowledge those strengths or keep it moving. We want to be praised and doted on. We want to be taken care of. We don't need to be taken care of, but women want it all the same.

A woman is willing to overlook many things, including unattractive physical attributes of a man and whatever else he lacks, if he makes her feel a certain way.

We are extremely emotional beings, so if a man makes a woman feel a certain way, he is guaranteed to win her over. It is emotions that can drive women to give a man her everything and make him the center of her world. Or, conversely, to leave him and seek emotional connection somewhere else. Because women need positive reassurance. We need to know that you understand our value. Just like we already understand it. And if you don't say it, you don't show it and we don't feel it, then that connection simply is not there, and we'll seek it elsewhere.

Modern society considers relationships and commitment as disposable. According to Time the divorce rate in the US has dropped to 39% , however, there is a decline the marriage rate as well as the cohabitation rate. More and more couples are fine just living together and never getting married. There is just not enough emphasis on building successful relationships that lead to marriage. Marriage is portrayed as a burden and sometimes meaningless. I've worked with couples where one wanted marriage, while the other partner compared the commitment to "just a piece of paper".

Relationships and marriage is seen as just a formality. And if you don't like it, end it, start all over and try again. That's not what relationships and commitment is all about. How can you fully commit to someone when you go into it with a mindset of "I don't have to be here?" That's what society shows people nowadays, that you don't have to be serious going into a relationship. You don't have to give it your all. Because if you don't like it, you don't have to be there. In effect, this kind of thinking makes relationships optional, not permanent.

A good relationship is a partnership. It is a strong one, where two people come together, willing to be fully committed, fully invested, and to stop at nothing to make it work. I think a real relationship doesn't have a finish line. It will never stop being worked on. It is a full-time, every day for the rest of your life commitment. And in a real relationship, people understand that you're going to have hard times, great times, and times where you want to give up. But in a real relationship where you feel like this is your everything, you fully commit and you invest yourself and do whatever it takes to make sure that the relationship is successful. And that's the true meaning and purpose of relationship.

In a relationship, I don't think there are specific roles a man has to take. I do, however, think there are specific characteristics a man should have. Every family has a different composition and method of operation. We have, for example, stay at home dads, and men who let the wife be the bread winner. And I don't think that's necessarily wrong because everybody's relationship is unique. But a man should still be a provider, protector and a leader. He can still lead his family as a man, even if he is not the financial provider. You can still provide and protect. A man has to be number one in his household because just like the game of chess, while the queen is the most powerful player on the board and can make the most moves, without the King, the game is over. It is the same thing in a family where the King essentially is needed. Just like that game, a man shall lead his family, provide for his family and protect his family.

So, even while the roles may be different in every family, the characteristics of the relationship remain the same. Once again in a relationship, there are no specific roles, however, when it comes to a woman there are certain characteristis she has to offer. We are naturally nurtering. Just as you would expect your husband to provide regardless of his job title, it is your job to provide nurture. Now, for example, I'm a stay at home mom, so I am often taking care of everyone else in my family. However, there are times where im required to be even more nurturing. My family depends on me to be the one to care for and encourage them. There are double standards in this world and that's one of them. Not to say a man can't be a nurturer but we are just better at it. And regardless of your situation or your family dynamic, that is something that is ultimately the woman's responsibility.

In addition to being the family nurturer It is very important that no matter the family orientation that you allow your man to feel like a man. Even if you're the bread winner, you understand that your husband is still a man, and your partner has needs.

Never forget that you freely decided to take on that role. This where women have to pick up more slack in the relationship, this will be where the scales may be a little unbalanced. Don't fret there will definitely be areas in the relationship where he has to give more as well.

Another characteristic, which might make some women cringe but is very necessary is the need for compliance. It is important for a woman to show that not everything has to be about her. We can be very dominating and overbearing. There is a time and place for that behavior, but in your relationship you must master the fine art of biting your tongue. Learn when it's a good time to maturly and firmly express yourself as opposed to the time when you need to shut up and listen. Remember when your are talking, you are teaching. When you are listening you are learning. You want to make your man feel like he's the leader, regardless of whatever his official role is.

Allow your man to be just that, a man. If you aren't confident in his abilities tolead you and your family then you shouldn't be with him. Now this is within a very specific context because allowing him to make all the decisions is unrealistic. But make him feel like he has a say, like you value his opinion, because uo should.

For Example, I do all the decorating in our home. Although I know my husband could care less what color pillows I purchase I still include him in the decision making. Nine times out of ten, he picks whatever I've picked but he was still included. Its small gestures like that, that men get off on. Now I know that his opinion changed nothing and I got what I wanted but he FELT like he had a say. Im telling you those little things make a difference.

Another example is say after a long day at work you come home super tired.

The only thing on your mind is a hot bath and your cozy bed. But that the furthest thing from his mind because hes expecting you to "perform". As frustrating as it may be there are times you will need to put his needs before your own. In this example I advise you to compromise without him knowing. Give in tohim but make it short. Most women know exactly how to get their man where he needs to be in a timely fashion. Then tend to your needs and end the night with everyone feeling satisfied.

15

Men are very physical beings. If you know your man needs some sexual attention, make sure he is no only emotionally fulfilled but sexually as well. When a man is not fulfilled, he's going to wander. That's just the way it is. Every relationship has stress. Every relationship is going to face many obstacles. But when two are putting the betterment of your relationship at the forefront of your priorities then you will have success.

The key to a successful relationship/marriage is communication. Most people try to run the relationship purely on love. That would be great if that's all it took to have a great long lasting relationship. But what does love have to do with it if you cannot communicate with one another? Good communication leads to everything else. If you can't talk to me, you can't tell me how you feel. You can't express your feelings. Futhermore, trust, love, loyalty and longevity comes from learning each other. That does not happen without effective communication.

A lot of marriages and relationships are not successful, because that line of communication is not open. Simply talking to each other is different than communicating. When you are communicating with each other, you'll know it because you'll be able to approach every hurdle with complete confidence that you can go to your partner.

A man really needs to be treated like you would treat a little boy. Boys are insecure, not really sure of themselves, still trying to figure things out. It is a known fact that girls mature at a faster pace than boys. Let's just keep it real men are never fully going to reach the same maturity as a woman.

As I alluded to in the early part of this chapter, treat your man the exact same way you would treat your third-grade kid. Take my son for example, I could give hime detailed step-by-step instructions and he'll come back and he may have completed one. The same with my husband. I can send my husband to the store with a list, with the exact brand, color and size of each item. It is aguarantee that he will get something wrong. We criticize men harder because they're bigger and

ARIANE ROBINSON

they're expected to know more, but the truth is, they really don't.

<u>CHAPTER TWO</u>

Nowadays with online dating and social media, a woman can get on Match.com, Plenty of Fish, or even Instagram, and easily meet men. Simply leaving the house, going to the gym, the grocery store, picking your kids up from school, you can meet a man. Realistically, it's not hard for a woman to get the attention of a man. I mean, it's just nature. Men usually are set up to chase, and to lust for a woman.

What you must understand is, there's somebody for everybody. Men love 'em all. If you're short, tall, big, small, there's a man out there somewhere that loves you. And if you don't believe me, watch "My 600 Pound Life." There are men out there that will love every fold and crevice of

your body. If you're short there is a man out there that loves you, too; there's somebody for every person whether you are dark, light, tall, wear glasses, white, black, Asian, any race, any height, any size, any stature. There's somebody for you. Once you make yourself available and you open up to dating good news is you wnt have to wait long before getting male attention. Now finding a good man is a different story.

I'm a little traditional. So, if it was up to me, I would say meeting a man organically would be the best way to go. However, I do understand that times have changed and we must acclaimate to changes. You know, back in the day you would go to your church, your school, or rely on your hobbies.

For example, if you are a bowler and you are a part of a bowling league, naturally at the bowling alley, you're going to find people and men who share that same interest with you.

I would certainly recommend that, but in this day and age, when it comes to the more modern approaches, I say, "If you can't beat, join them"! Get on social media, pay for the online dating subscriptions. Take the time to get on these websites, set up profiles and explore all of your options.

The truth is, the dating process has been simplified. Now you can literally be looking for men online while relaxing on your couch. That's right, you don't even have to leave your house. There are many benefits to the modern way of dating. One is some dating sites offer background checks which is helpful when you're opening up to different men, you want to weed out the creeps upfront. Another benefit is you can see his hobbies and interests and even see if you are compatable prior to initiating a conversation.

It removes the need of going on the dates and first day, second day, third day to find out that you and this man don't have anything in common. I recommend opening yourself up in all facets and being open to different ways of meeting a new man.

Once you're open to dating it's important for every woman to have a checklist of what she's looking for in a man. You must judge a book by its cover, come on don't act like you don't do this already. When you're dating and you're putting yourself in a vulnerable place. So, you want to be certain that you aren't being too open by passing out your number or replying to every dm or email unproductively. You should always use reasonable discretion when dating. And if you are systematic about it and know exactly what you're looking for, then there is no time to play games with any kind of nonsense.

Any man that you come in contact with, judge him. Look at his haircut, how he's dressed, how well-groomed he is. Of course, that's not to say, for example, that a man who just got off of work from a construction site doesn't deserve your number. But if you have a list of what you are looking for then you will know if a man meets your requirements or not.

Pay close attention to how polite he is, how he addresses, if he opens your door and looks you in yours eyes. These are all things that we need to be very serious about while looking for a man. When you are looking at a man you can tell a lot about him. Pay attention to his hair, the way he smells, his skin, if he has clean hands, if his clothing is properly fitting. If it appears that he hasn't had a haircut in a while, he has an odor or his clothes are too worn, then those are all indications of his hygiene.

What you see is what you get. If you like what you see, persue him. If not don't hesitate to keep it moving.

Dating opens you up to a lot of all kinds of people, some favorable and some not. So, just as you wouldn't walk down the street, wearing a tee shirt with your phone number on it. You need to be very guarded with the information that you pass out online as well.

That's why I said to have a list. Some examples may included physical attributes, age, personality qualities, etc. Having a checklist makes meeting new men a smooth process. With your list you'll be prepared to either move forward with dating a new man or identify the lack of requirements and cut it off. The whole object of dating is to meet and interact with men that are suitable for marriage, according to your guidelines.

You're looking for a life partner, therefore you judge everything about this man. I'm not saying people don't have a bad day, but this man is supposed to be putting his best foot forward on a date. Therefore, if he couldn't take the time out to get a fresh haircut, clip his nails, smell good and look good, then that's the first indication that there is a problem. After all, I'm sure you dressed to a tee to impress him. Why didn't he do the same for you?

It may seem very childish to look at these things, but it's actually quite important. You have no time to waste; time waits for no one. And if you're looking for your partner, these are the things you need to judge up front. Don't wait down the line to go on a third and fourth date, giving him a pass on day one only to later find out that he is not the man for you.

Don't be ackward but be very observant. This is where you should be checking off some of those requirements on your list.

If you meet a man with slumped shoulders who holds his head down and is soft spoken and some of your requirements is dominance and confidence, then you will know right from the beginning that this man is not for you.

One requirement that makes most womens list is a man's position in life. Depending on what age group you are in, of course, will dictate your own requirement of where you believe he should be in life. But the problem is, society makes you think that if a man has a good paying or is a certain level in lifethat he's instantly a good catch. However, a man's income or choice of car is not always a direct reflection of a man's character.

I'm sure most women have experience the situation when you tell your friends you are dating someone new. The first questions are "Oh, girl, where does he work? How much does he make, what car does he drive?"

All of these are good questions but , are merely superficial things that really don't describe the core of a man. Society really has portrayed a false sense of what a real man is.

A well off, abusive asshole is not a good man, because he has money and nice things. Having a good job does not automatically make you an ideal catch. Driving a BMW does not automatically make a man a "keeper." Society puts too much emphasis on the external, to the point where women are not even digging deeper to see what this man is all about prior to investing their time and energy. No wonder there are so many failed relationships and marriages these days, when they're built on such shaky foundations.

A man should have a job, preferably a nice job. He should be more accomplished, depending on what age group he is in. On the other hand a man should also be intelligent, have drive and ambition.

You can always build up a man. In fact, men need to be built up. When the right man and woman and come together, that's when you get a power couple. They say behind every good man is a strong woman.

That is indeed a fact. Your new man may not be an executive or have a luxury car, but he may in transition in his life. He may just be waiting on his queen to unlock his true potential. Be prepared to put in some work, your new man may need your assistance in pulling out the best in him. Polish that diamond Girl!

In order to really label a man as a good catch, you need to dig a little deeper than that and go beyond just the external. You need to see what's really in the core of that man. Does he have what it takes to really build a future with you? Remember, this has nothing to do with what position he holds at his job or what kind of car he drives.

On the other hand, society labels a good woman as an independent woman. Strong women that don't need or want a man. Now there is nothing wrong with being independent and confident in your abilities to survive on your own. But that does not mean that we don't desire companionship. I've never met a woman who wanted to die alone. We are not being set up to have happy, successful relationships.

Now as we carry-on with our checklists, which is indeed essential, be certain to set those same standards for yourself. As women, we have no problem being vocal about what we will and will not accept. But what do *you* bring to the table? It's not good enough to have a nice body and keep your hair and nails done. So you paid your own bills and maintained your lifestyle while you were single. That's what you should've done. Now you're dating and want

A man to subtract your problems and add to your pockets, but what do you offer him? As society paints its own picture of an ideal woman, realize that image severely differs from what men desire. And it is up to us women, to change that.

It is critical to realize that what you've accomplished in life for your self does not automatically make you wife material. Just as you are judging every aspect of a man, you should be prepared to go under that same microscope. Don't be ignorant to think that you have no room for improvement. Work on yourself and offer the same qualities and characters you are asking for, regardless of what it what society says is trending right now.

If you're still dating, go hard at it, your man is out there. If you've found your man and you both are knocking things off your checklists' and are equally interested in each other, Congratulations! You have potenttially found your future husband. Now it's time to work on keeping him.

<u>CHAPTER THREE</u>

ARAINE ROBINSON

So, you found your man! You guys are getting to
know each other, figuring out each other's likes and
dislikes, learning all the expectations and deal breakers
in the relationship. Finding out if you both want kids or
deciding the right time to introduce your new man to
your kids or vice versa. Understand this is an important
time. This is the time you're building your foundation.
If you have a weak foundation, any structure will fall,
and relationships are included in that.

In the beginning stages of your relationship, you
definitely want to interact as much as possible.

Communication is one of the most important
aspects of a relationship, so that's something you need
to do constantly and as frequently as possible.
Communication is not just calling or physically standing
in each other's faces. There are many different avenues
you can use to communicate.

Send him a good morning text in the morning,
call him on your ride to work, mix it up a little bit, go on
his social media and send him a a DM. Stay relevant in

32

his mind. You definitely don't want to leave too much free time for him to entertain another woman who is showing more interest than you are. It doesn't have to be the same thing every day. Text him "good morning" today, tomorrow call him during your lunch break or during his lunch break just to see how his day's going. However you go about it, you definitely want to keep your interaction with him very frequent.

Don't cross over the line into stalking this man because you don't want to scare him off. But you do want him to see that you are interested in him. You both need to see and feel just how invested you both are in this new relationship.

As adults it is very easy to let life get in the way of making time for your man. You're in the beginning stages of this relationship, and it is very critical to continue to date each other. There's no certain number of dates you need to go on every month in your relationship, but it should be as many as you can, as this is likely to have a profound effect on your success. Your dates don't have to be expensive. If you are already cooking dinner, light a couple candles, sit at the table, talk to each other, turn off your cell phones, turn the TV off and just really interact with each other. It should be of high-priority to not only connect physically, but mentally and spiritually as well.

And you can't do that if you're not spending time with each other.

You don't have to do too much. Go to the beach, lay some blankets out and talk about your childhoods, or just listen to the water crash. Go to the park and play cards. Tell each other jokes or watch a new series on Netflix. That's the stuff that builds great relationships. A date doesn't need to be expensive and stressful. A dates to Red Lobster or Mr. Chow is nice. But when the emphasis is put on the value of the date as opposed to the significance of being together,then you're wasting your time in the relationship. Set your own standards but the main focus should be spending time together and that can happen anywhere.

This foundation is set when you two are just genuinely enjoying each other's company, whether it be at the fanciest of restaurants or your backyard under the stars.

You may have expensive taste and want nothing but the best, there's nothing wrong with that. However, don't be so high maintanence that you miss opportunities to further your relationship because you can't dine at a place up to your standards.

Many people think that once they have gotten a partner that the hard work stops. And that couldn't be any farther from the truth. That's when the real work begins. Don't forget there will be busy times where you can't make it out to dinner or a movies, however, alone time is still necessary. Lay a blanket out and have a picnic in the living room. When my husband and I started dating finances were heavily guarded.

There were times that we picked up takeout and chilled at home and there were times that we could afford to splurge and we did it big.

Either way, we reminisce on those times as some of the best times of our lives. To start from the very beginning. As I stated, that foundation has to be solid.

It is important to keep in mind exactly what the end goal is. The goal is not to keep having a better date each time. The goal is to really understand each other, to learn about each other more and more as the days pass. How can you make this man happy and fulfill him if you don't even know him? You might like his body, he might look good, but what's in his mind? What is he thinking? How does he really operate? That's the stuff you learn when you date each other. To this day, I still date my husband. We've been married almost 10 years married now. We never stopped dating. Even if that means putting the kids to bed, making drinks and just talking until we fall asleep.

The goal is never to just have a man. But to find a good man worthy of having you and building a healthy, happy, forever lasting relationship. In order to do that it is imperative that you make the time to learn each other.

Whether it be five minutes or a whole weekend, every moment spent together is an investment into the future of your relationship. It is said that absence makes the heart grow fonder. Well that does not apply to a relationship in its early stages.

Time is something that we aren't guaranteed. With that being said you should see to it that you spend as much time as you can with your man. If you find yourself needing too much alone time, then you should probably just be alone.

If you're reading this book, it's strong possibility that you've probably kissed a few frogs already. So, kissing is probably not that big of a deal to you. You'd be surprised to find that many woman frequently question the right time to kiss or share any type of intimacy with a new man. Understand that you're still allowing somebody into your personal space and that's still intimacy no matter how you look at it.

If in previous relationships you allowed intimacy early on in the relationship and those relationships did not work out, then I advise you to do things differently this time around. Only a fool does the same action expecting a different result.

Sis, there are still diseases out there. You surely want to be selective if and when you're planning on engaging in any kind of intimacy.

People do kiss on the first date. And there's nothing wrong with that. If you felt an instant connection, go for it! But if not, then that's something with which you can take your time.Far too often we jump into physical contact before we get to know the mental and emotional aspects of relationships, and that's something that needs to be guarded much more closely.

Lets just get right into "it" and by "it", I mean sex. If you feel like busting it wide open on the first date, by all means do so, but understand what tone you're setting for your relationship. There is no right or wrong way to approach intimacy in a new relationship. Do you. You are a grown woman. Nobody can tell you when you should feel comfortable or be ready to have sex with this man for the first time. With that being said, you don't want this man to stick around because of what you did on the first night. That's not what you're trying to set up.

That's not the foundation you're trying to lay; remember you're trying to establish a true relationship. You're trying to keep this man around. Your tricks can wait a little bit, but to each his own.

Remember your body is your temple. If you are not really certain about the direction yet and you guys haven't really built up that strong connection, there is no reason why you should be letting this man into your temple. A man can go out and get sex from pretty much anywhere, just like a woman. Understand if you want this man, there are a hundred other women lined up waiting for him too. The qualities you see in this man are the same things that another woman will see and want.

You need him to be emotionally and mentally connected as well. So, wait until there's a little connection there.

That could be after the first date. That could be after two or three months. There is no certain time. But if you two are really connected, that man will wait as long as you want him to.

Show him why you're the best woman for him. Sex doesn't really have that much to do with that. Now don't get it twisted. Sex is a big part of arelationship, but it's not the biggest part of a relationship. You two need to really know each other, understand each other and by the time you really get to sex after all of that, that's going to be the best sex you've ever. As you already know when you have the total package and there are emotions involved and you really get each other, the sex is so intense.

When you connect with this man and you really have that chemistry and you really have that interest now, it's not just lust. It's not just sex.

It turns into making love, contributing to that strong foundation. Sex should never supercede actual relatioinship building. Any woman can get him there. If he needs to, he can even get himself there. But why should he want you to get him there? Why should you be the woman to take him into that place and vice versa?

Guard your temple. Because every man shouldn't be able to experience you. You are not a "Hot and Ready" and shouldn't be readily available to any man. We all have needs, but don't let that get in the way of what you're really trying to set up because nowadays with $40 a man can afford a happy ending.

You are trying to build something Special. Trying to get this man and keep him. That needs to be your main focus, not sex.

"I love you." Those are very powerful words. Those are not casual words to be used to fancy a man. I'm sure you don't run around just telling people you hate them and you shouldn't be quick to say you love too many people, especially in the beginning stages of dating. Love means an intense feeling of deep affection. Some people are excessively affectionate and develop feelings rather early on. While others take much longer to discover these emotions. Be certain to never play on these words.

Now, there is a such thing as love at first sight. There are some people who have looked at another person and knew, without a doubt, that they were meant to be together. However, loving someone at first sight and being in love with a person is two different things.

Once there's a connection established and you are willing to drop everybody and anybody that gets in the way of our relationship, when you're willing to stop at nothing (reasonable) to make sure that this is a successful relationship, then it is probably safe to say that you are in love. Love is not just a word, it must be back with deep emotions.

So, you have been dating and spending lots of time together, connecting mentally and probably physically, expressing your love for one another, and now you are thinking about living together.

Many different factors come into play when you consider living together. There are different hurdles to face such as, introducing kids if either or both of you have them. Figuring out whose you two in live in? If you

both agree on having pets and or if you'll live in the inner city or suburbs.

It's easy to hide who you really are when you're just visiting each other. During those visits you may notice that he keeps his house clean, he always has groceries, and he seems to be organized. Yeah, that's real cute until you see the other side! When you are living with each other you get the raw un-cut version of your partner. That's when you will see him after he's let his guard. Living together removes the veil real quick. It's all cute until you're tripping over his dirty drawers and he forgets to rinse the sink out after he brushes his teeth.

There are more serious issues to address as well. As I stated previously, if there are children involved, they need to be considered as well. You should know prior to moving in what role he would play in your kid(s) daily lives and how he would approach disciplining them.

There are also decisions to be made on who will be responsible for the bills and how the division of household responsibilities will be split. There are just so many different factors to take into consideration when it comes to living together.

With all that being stated, most couples decide to live together prior to marriage. There are many benefits to this arrangement. The main benefit being you literally get to experience what married life will look like with your partner. The main negative is, men get comfortable relatively easy. If he has everything desired prior to marriage he may question "If it's not broke, why fix it."

44

If you decide to go the more traditional route and wait until after marriage that decision as well, comes with both positive and negative results. Just understand that you said, "for better or for worse."

So, it doesn't matter what you're getting when you move your stuff into that place. You told God and your new spouse that you're going to take it, you're going to accept whatever comes.

I personally think that it is very important to not delay this step too long. When you know what you want, I say, go for it. If he's made it this far chances are you are planning on having a future with him. Don't delay the inevitable. Introduce him to the kids and family and make strides towards your future. Why wait years down the line to figure out you've wasted time with a man that doesn't get along with your kids?

The timeframe is really your own to make. However, remember, time will not pause while you figure it out. That's why it is so important in the beginning to lay it all out there.

You don't want to prolong the decision just to find out later that he hates your family pet or that he expects you to pay half of all the bills while you were expecting him to carry that load.

That's for you in your own individual relationship to decide how fast you are going to move. Because once you both determine that this is what you want, then you need to be actively, progressively moving ahead in your relationship. And unless you two are the rare couple that decides you're never going to live together, then it's going to inevitably happen.

If you have taken the leap and decided to live together, the next step is to begin putting forth the effort to execute the plans you both made for your future together.

CHAPTER FOUR

Like I stated in chapter one, if left to chance, most men will cheat. If we are not happy, we will leave. There is no way we will stick around too long if it's something we are just totally against, there are some exceptions to the rule, but we will leave before we lead a double life. Men are different, they will stay in an unhealthy relationship where they are not fully satisfied and go and get their needs met by somebody else.

It is important to understand that if you're not going to satisfy your man, then there is a strong possibility that he will seek satisfaction elsewhere.

Let me be very clear, it's never our fault why he cheated. As women, we should never blame ourselves for a man not doing what he has committed himself to do. However, as women, we also need to understand our power and understand our roles in our relationships.

It is crucial that you fully comprehend what role you play in keeping your man on the right track and keeping him faithful. If in the beginning, you both expressed your needs, wants and expectations of your relationship, then you should be aware of what he is expecting. If one of his expectations were a hot homecooked meal when he gets home from work, and you agreed, then more days then none he should have his hot meal waiting on him. It's a little late in the game to now decide, once you have a man, that you don't want to do what it takes to maintain the relationship.

Remember, men are like kids. To make matters worse, they respond like kids by throwing temper tantrums. Cheating is just a man's way of throwing a temper tantrum because he is unhappy. As women, like I said, we get unhappy. Guess what? We may curse him out and yell a bit, but after that, he is kicked to the curb.

Men just don't respond that way. They will live a double life. They will go do their dirt and come home and lay next to you.

Believe it or not there are women who will happily play side chick. She will not mind getting a fraction of your man as opposed to having a whole bum.

Morals are a thing of the past when it comes to those women. In their minds his vows are not her commitment. And although that is true, when we must help keep our men focused.

Men don't process stress in the way that we do and don't handle it the same way we do. They don't deal will with disagreements and frequent arguing. A simple debate about putting the toilet seat down is seen as nagging to them. Continuous arguing paired with your lack of desire to please him will start the countdown to when he will stray.

Unfortunately cheating has become a standard practice and many couples deal with the consequences of such actions. Stay strong in your relationship and keep him interested and fulfilled. It may feel like you carry most of the weight, but you are doing what best for you and your relationship. Don't forget that you chose this man.

That does not mean become his slave. Rather do what you can when you can. Keeping your relationship on track should be your focus, not how strenuous it can be. Keep in mind that this is all for your benefit as well.

In relationships men need to that they have something of value. No man is going to respect and value a woman that does not value and respect herself. No man should like he settled for the woman he is with. Or that he can do better. Having a pretty face and nice body is not enough, just ask all the beautiful women with broken hearts.

It should be your mission to continuously show your man the phenomenal woman you. Keep him intrigued by you. You want your man to feel like he won the ultimate prize by having you.

He needs to understand what he has and what he stands to lose. A healthy amount of fear is necessary. If he doesn't fear losing you, he will not put much effort into keeping you. It will not matter to if you're with him or not. If he doesn't fear losing you, then the relationship is already at a loss.

He needs to understand that you contribute way too much and that his life would change too drastically if you weren't in it. That one night with another woman not worth all that he stands to lose with you.

It is said that, what's done in the dark, will come to light, and that is so true. However, I am not the type to just sit around and wait for it to come to me. I am going to find it! Trust your intuition. If you feel like something is wrong, then it most likely is. This is your relationship, your life, your future we're talking about. So, if you think he's cheating, chances are, he is.

There is no reason for serious secrets in a relationship. For example, if you don't know the password to your man's phone, you're already off to a bad start. There should be nothing in that phone that you can't see.

Text messages, emails, pictures, nothing. If he has a password on his phone that he refuses to tell you, he's hiding something. My husband isn't allowed to have a pass code, a pin code, a zip code, or any code that I don't know.

There is no need for that kind of privacy. You want some privacy? Go use the bathroom. You can shut the door. I don't even want you to lock it in case I need to come in. If a man is "allowed" to come and go as he pleases, keep secrets from you and make decisions based off his own feelings, he most definitely will do just that.

For business, my husband's phone must be locked, but guess what? I know that passcode and he better not even look at me too fast when I pick up his phone.

I get mixed feedback on this topic. Some women make checking up on their man apart of their daily routine. While others take a more laid-back approach and hope for the best. Stop with all the BS thinking only jealous women keep tabs on their men. No, that's what smart women do. When you know better you do better. I'm sure there are past situations that you look back on with regret or guilt. Wishing that you could change the outcome, if only you had been more aware. Well here is your chance.

Furthermore, you should not give a damn what anyone has to say about how you conduct your healthy relationship. Hell, I search my kids' backpacks at the end out the day and monitor their phones and internet use, just to make sure they are constantly focused on the right things and not getting into any trouble. Why should it be any different with my man?

Well, I'm searching my man's pants pockets. Reading receipts and checking bank accounts. I know what he likes to eat and where he shops, so I'll easily recognize if something is out of the ordinary. This is not something that consumes me or prevents me from leading a normal life. This is just an added effort I put forth to secure the longevity of my union.

By no means does this guarantee that your man won't get stuff pass you. Although it does provide him with additional healthy fear. He should never think that you are too busy with your life to see what he's hiding from you.

On the other hand, I am a completely open book. My husband has access to all my passwords, codes and pins as well. I have nothing to hide and I am happy to provide my man with the security of knowing he has nothing to worry about. We discuss how we feel about each other's friends and behaviors. No one outside my marriage is more important than my husband.

You should not be with a man that you have to hide things from. If you need secrets in your relationship, you need to be single because there's nothing that your partner should not be able to know about you. I understand privacy. But, privacy in a relationship should not go beyond, alone time in the bathroom. Going to get a mani/pedi is a nice way to get alone time or going out with your girlfriends.

When it comes to anything else, you both need to be as involved with each other as possible. If you keep him on his toes and limit secrets and separation, the likelihood of him cheating is slim to none.

Leave no room for any errors. There should be no time to think about another woman because when he is not with you, he's thinking about you, while you are checking in on him. A confident, secure man that puts his relationship first will see no problem in you knowing what's going on with him.

Just for the record, keeping up with your man does not mean that you don't trust him or that you are jealous. It indicates that you understand how this world operates. That the evils of this world will invade your relationship the moment you drop your guard.

My husband and I have been married almost ten years and I practice what I preach.

To this day I still keep tabs on him. I still checking our bank accounts, messages and receipts. Thankfully, we have never dealt with any kind of infidelities in our relationship. I trust my husband, but that's where the trust begins and ends.

By no means do we have a controlling relationship. What we have is a transparent relationship. Society makes you think you're supposed to be two separate people. No, we are one. If I have a pass code, WE have a pass code. If I have a debit card, WE have a debit card. The same security I expect is the same security I offer.

You need to study your man and your relationship like you're about to take the hardest test of your life. You wouldn't go into a college course and not study, knowing that this determines whether you get your degree.

You should study your man because the success of your relationship should be one of the most important priorities in your life. Take the time to learn everything about your man.

You should know his friends; you can tell a lot about him by the company he keeps. If his friends are all committed men that enjoys an occasional night at the golf course, know that. If his friends are a bunch of bachelors that like to bar hop, you need to know that as well. Knowledge is power.

If you are a woman that prefers to take the laid-back approach and hope for the best, that is your prerogative. That may work for you; however, I still recommend that you pay attention to simple signs that you don't have to do much investigating to see. If he hides his phone from you, prefers to be out with his friends and/or does not communicate freely, you may have a major problem on your hands.

The operation of your relationship is your business. If you decide to deal with a cheating man, that is your choice to make. Whatever you chose, don't be a fool and allow this man to just entertain space in your life, woman up and take control of what you want. We are all grown women here. If you had a man or successful relationship, there would be no need for this book. It's time to get your man and be successful at it.

Every relationship is different. If you experience infidelity you are faced with making a hard, life changing decision. To stay or to leave. I have worked with couples who have dealt with infidelity in some form and stayed in the relationship.

In one case the woman felt as if she failed her man and bared the burden of guilt. She felt that her fiancé's need to cheat was her fault. She stayed and forgave him. That was her call to make and there is no right or wrong decision.

I personally don't feel that any woman should fault themselves for a grown man neglect his commitment and responsibilities. There are always things we can do better; however, an unfaithful man should carry the weight of his failure all on his own.

From day one, if you are giving your all, putting everything you've got into this relationship and making the best effort to fully fulfill not only your man, then there is no reason why a man should get away with cheating. You deserve better than that.

Don't get it twisted. I do believe that men can change. People make mistakes. Every woman has to evaluate her own individual situation and decide if it is too detrimental to stay.

In my personal relationship, my husband knows that cheating completely unacceptable. That infidelity is terms for termination of our relationship. I have always been very clear about my stance on this issue.

People like to be cute and say that they have unconditional love for their spouse and that's just a whole load of BS. In most situations love is conditional. I will love my spouse with all my heart only if he does not hurt me, devalue and abuse me.

Cheating is a form of mental abuse. If you are a woman who has ever been lied to, cheated on or heart broken you know what that does to you. You understand the sleepless nights, inability to eat, and the mental damper and strain it puts on you.

Its ok to have conditions on your love. Its ok to have deal breakers and to be firm in your decision to not accept crap just to have a man. You can do bad all by yourself, a man should add to your wellbeing, not multiply problems.

With all that being said, I put my everything into my relationship, I hold nothing back. I aim to please my man. Why? Because I think it's important for me to not only understand my feelings and needs and wants, but I need to understand his as well. Being a grown woman in a relationship, I play a big part in the success of my relationship.

If you notice the signs that your man is unhappy or considering stepping out, you need to talk to him. Communicate your concerns and reiterate your deal breakers. The last thing you want is to have a serious issue take place and because you haven't decided where you stand on the issue, you're forced to make a lifetime decision while emotionally and mentally impaired.

If he has cheated, and you decide to stay, it is important to understand why he did it in the beginning. Once all factors have been considered and you work through all the issues, you may never have a problem again. That is a possibility. But if he was able to find a loophole to get away with it the first time and you don't change how you operate in the relationship, then he may try it again.

Also consider it is crucial to consider all possible ramifications attached to his infidelity. Consider how you would respond if year later; after you repaired the trust and moved on, a woman contacts you looking for her baby daddy. How would you deal with being surprised with a baby your man created with another woman? Would you stay and help him raise that child, or would that be the straw that broke the camel's back?

You must do what's best for your relationship but pay attention to everything that's going on around you. For every example I provided, there is a woman who has experienced it and, make no doubt about it, you do not want to be that woman.

A woman should never settle in her relationship and give up her dreams and expectations of what she wants for her future just because she has a man. By no means am I saying just having a man is good enough. Absolutely not. If you have always dreamed of being married and planned a life with kids and a house with a red door and white picket fence, never give up on that.

If you ever looked at other couples' failures or shortcomings and proclaimed to never be that woman, don't be that woman. There is no reason to completely trade in all your dreams for a man ok with playing house forever. Or to settle with a man that treats you like shit.

As I previously stated, there's somebody for everybody, and if that man is not willing to give you commitment and fulfill your dreams (Within reason), then perhaps you skipped a couple steps. A man that values you as his queen will want you to be his wife. He will want to spend the rest of his life protecting and providing for you. You should not have to convince your man to marry you, the right man will want to.

<u>Chapter Five</u>

The traditional family dynamic has drastically changed. Once forbidden lifestyles and genres of sexuality are now acceptable and welcomed. Naturally this makes dating and finding compatibility more difficult.

I hear a lot of women say there is a shortage of good men. And although it may feel that way, the truth is there are plenty of available men, they just aren't considered good men.

For example, there are some good men locked up in prison for dumb crimes, especially in the black community.

There are men serving time right now for unpaid parking tickets or for making a mistake as a teen. Men are being locked up at a rapid rate and some for minor crimes, non-violent crimes. There are men who spent decades behind bars just to be released due to being wrongfully convicted.

Then, once this man is released from jail, who wants him? He's instantly pegged a bad guy. We tell ourselves we don't want the project of fixing a man.

We want to find a man who is already prepared for us to take in. However, that's not always realistic. There are good men who are dressed in bad clothing. It is what it is. That kind of baggage is not easy to look past. There are other causes for the shortage as well. Such as the undercover down-low brothers and the immature men that want to be a playboy and never settle down.

Social media and reality tv play a big part in this. All over reality TV, we're seeing these down-low brothers, guys who play on the other side, bad boys, families being torn apart by men who just want to be players and so on. The marriage rate has decreased, and more and more children are being raised in broken families and with absent fathers.

So, where do they get their real example of true commitment? Who's teaching these boys how to be good family men, how to treat a woman and how to lead a family? Therefore, these boys become men who don't know how to conduct themselves as real men.

There are songs out there telling us that "you can't raise a man". Well, you can do is teach him. At the very least you must be willing to take on a project. A diamond may not always shine.

Now please don't rush down to your local homeless shelter or prison looking for your diamond in the ruff. I am saying what you are looking for may not come in the package you anticipate.

We must change our perceptions of men. If you can't seem to find exactly what you are looking for or you've had previous relationships that failed, perhaps you are interested in the wrong kind of guys anyway. Just like we have to build ourselves up, we may have to build them up as well. There is nothing wrong with that.

Now on to another issue. No matter what situation you are presented with in your relationship, with preparation, you can get through it. If in the beginning you laid out exactly what you expect out of the relationship and what the goals are, then he should already know exactly how long the dating phase will last and when you'll be ready to be married.

After finding the right man or molding an okay man into your dream man, facing all awkwardness a new relationship can pose, you do not want to be faced with the repercussions of not communicating. By maintaining constant communication, you avoid having to present your partner with ultimatums. If it comes to a point where you feel as if you need to give an ultimatum, then you haven't built this relationship on a solid foundation. He should have known, from the time you two became serious, your timeline to marriage.

Why go into a relationship with blind expectations? If you failed to express your desire to be married within a certain amount of time then, of course you would feel the need to give him an ultimatum. If you chose to wait it out and see how things go, then you can't blame him if he takes it time. If you laid all the terms out in all your expectations, then if he fails to accommodate that request, the fault is his. And you won't need to give him an ultimatum. The failure to commit to you is him showing that marriage is not what he wants at that time.

If you never made that commitment a priority and was fine with playing house previously, it is unfair to expect him to read your mind and conform to your new ideal relationship. Have a clear cut plan and pursue it. Remain aware that while you're letting this man play games somebody else is on their way down the aisle. If you feel as if you need an ultimatum, then you skipped a couple of steps sis, go back and try again.

The bottom line is; if it comes to the point where you feel as if you need to give him an ultimatum of marry me or leave, then you have some serious decisions to make. He should want to secure you as his wife. This is something he should be happy to do. To me, an ultimatum is trying to force him into something for which he is not ready.

As women, we are extremely strong beings. We're independent, we're problem solvers and there is no challenge we can't face. With that being said, we should never be afraid to be alone. If it comes to a point where you have had relationships and they did not work out, that means you need some time alone. It is time for some soul searching.

It is ok to be selfish and to put yourself before anyone else. Even as moms, we care for our kids to no avail. We will make sacrifice after sacrifice and run ourselves into the ground. You can still be a good mom and put yourself first. If you are not good you can't be good for others, including you kids or a man.

Often when you jump into relationships too fast, you are looking for somebody else to make you happy. When you don't even know how to make yourself happy; you want somebody else to give you love because you don't love yourself. Furthermore, when you are alone, it gives you time to really learn yourself, to truly change, to heal and to figure out exactly what you're looking for.

Then when you re-enter the dating world you will know these things. Nobody can tell you anything about yourself. You'll be able to tell this man, I need X, Y, and Z, and be confident in your decisions. It should never be a time where you're afraid to be alone. Embrace it. Don't rush it. Work through it.

A lot of us women have unresolved issues from previous situations. Whether it be childhood traumas, daddy issues or old abusive relationships we tend to hold on to our baggage.

Far too often women are staying in relationships that are just not healthy. Have you ever witnessed a woman in an abusive relationship and wondered why she stayed? Well, I will answer that, because she was already broken. Because she was not mentally strong enough to put herself above that. Because she did not believe she deserved more. All of those reasons are usually a direct result of unhealed and unresolved trauma.

I have worked with women who were in abusive relationships. The common denominator was that they were all damaged goods. Understand, if you don't love yourself you are not in a position to give love and should not be in a relationship.

It is never your fault that someone does not understand your value or if someone is abusive to you, but it is your fault if you stay and allow it. There comes a time where you must heal and move on.

Take however much time you need and work through all your baggage. Work on regaining your confidence. I don't care what you failed in the past or how many accomplishments you have or lack. No one should ever be able to take your confidence, put their hands on you, and then make you feel less than.

And as women we have to reclaim our strength, build ourselves up, build each other up and understand that by no means should you sacrifice yourself just to have a man. This book is not to tell you to run out and grab the first man you can get. This expert advice is to help build successful, happy, healthy relationships, and not one relationship that has any sort of abuse is happy, healthy, or even partially successful. Whatever is coming ahead is much better than what you have dealt with. Find strength in yourself and you must whole heartedly that you deserve more.

While in a healthy marriage or serious relationship, it is my expert opinion that no man should have a best friend of the opposite sex. Period. There is no reason why he should have a female best friend besides you. If he needs somebody outside you, then you are not doing something right.

I'm not going to go to my childhood best friend, a male, and spend a whole day with him while my husband is at work.

That same energy can be put into my husband. Naturally, we have different interests, so no woman is going to directly relate to a man and vice versa. With that being said, all friends should be of the same sex. If a man wants to talk about golf or sports, he should do that with another man. If he can make time to go out and hit a dinner and a movie it damn sure shouldn't be with another woman.

You think a man with a female friend has never checked her out or thought about being with her? Yeah right, a man will be a man. If she bend's over in a pair of see-through leggings, I'm sorry (not sorry), best friend or not, he is taking a peek.

If you have any time to spend with the opposite sex, it should be bonding and communicating with your partner. And that goes back to what I previously said.

You should know what your man is doing anytime he has free time. Ultimately, you can't trust anyone else besides your partner, unless it's your sister or your mama and hell, he shouldn't be spending too much time with them either.

If he wants a friend, he can get a male friend or go get a puppy. Dogs are a man's best friend, but he should not have a close female friend, period. Now, having female co-workers is different. He should not be afraid to speak to his female co-workers but he dang sure should not be having solo lunches with her.

Once again, if they have a long leash, they are inevitably going to see what they can get away with. If a woman is not his sister, his mom or aunt, then she has to go. There is no place for even a distant cousin people are crazy these days.

CHAPTER SIX

Once you secured your man and you are married, you have to know that your husband is now a round one draft pick for a lot of single women. We tend to think that a man wearing a wedding band is a deterrent for single women. Actually, it is quite the opposite. It's almost like an advertisement. It shows that your man is not afraid of commitment and that he was such a great guy that another woman took him off the market. That makes him more appealing to single.

Desperate single women see a married man as the total package. His marriage band should symbolize him being off the market.

Instead it represents that your man was not like the rest of these guys out here, that he wasn't afraid to commit. That he was something special. These women are tired of getting duds and don't want to do the work. They want that diamond you polished; they want your man.

Everybody sees LeBron as the best player in the game, but they don't see all the practice and all the hard work, and all the family time sacrificed. All the sore muscles, missed holidays and injuries. Nobody acknowledges that. It's the same in every marriage. Women set their sights on this nice, polished man who is well-groomed, treats his woman like a queen and knows that once he's done with work, to come home. They don't know that when his wife met him; he didn't have that job position, he drove a beater and lived in a small apartment with a roommate.

But his wife accepted all his flaws, put that battery in his back and polished him up.

Being a side chick is now considered the cool thing. It is praised as if that doesn't mean breaking up a home. There are songs about side chicks being ok with having a married man on selected days. I coached a young lady that expressed that she only dated married men. Her reasoning was when that man was away from his wife he didn't want to deal with stress and was a good time. She was ok celebrating Valentines day a couple days after the actual day. As appalling as it sounds, she felt that his vows were not here to uphold, which mean that she was not in the wrong.

There is nothing that a married woman can do to stop another woman from shooting her shot. I mean, to be honest, we can't even be mad at it. As we all know, it is hard out there for everyone, men and women to find a good partner. It really is up to your man to honor his vows.

To not allow any outside influence to deter him from being a faithful husband. Do not be confused, If a man does not want to be in a relationship, there is nothing you can do to keep him. But if you have an overall good guy that treasures his union, these steps combined with daily effort will help you keep your man interested and invested in only you. The key is to make sure that the marriage is solid enough that your man has no time to check for another woman.

When a man's home is taken care of, and whatever your roles are, you both fulfill them; then it doesn't matter what another woman does to get his attention. That man will be so blinded by your full, there'll be no more room on his plate.

There are some many negative forces in this world that will destroy you and your marriage if you let it.

Protect and water your relationship like a garden. Fertilize your garden with communication, honesty, loyalty and trust.

I'm not worried about what a woman can offer my husband because ultimately, she can offer whatever she wants to, he doesn't have to take it. If he accepts it, then we had a problem long before she came along. Men flirt with me all the time. I don't pay it any mind because I know what I have. I value what I have. And that's what you need to make sure your husband does with you. Make sure that he can't possibly see or entertain what they're offering, because he's so focused on coming home and making you happy.

If you've noticed that your man seems a little weak, or you feel as if there's a possibility of him giving into temptation or he's expressed that he's not happy; then a married woman, as a partner, there shouldn't be too much unwilling to do to change that.

Remember, if your man is not happy, that is a recipe for disaster. Same with you. Would you stay in a relationship with a man that promised to be everything you desired, then he decided that he no longer cared how you felt or what you needed? I'm pretty certain the answer to that is no.

Take to time to talk to each other and listen to each other. You don't want either of you to feel like the other person's needs don't matter. Men are quick to build that wall. Men are not as emotional as women, so when you can pull a little emotion out and get him to communicate his feelings, appreciate that. Don't be self-centered thinking that it's always about your feelings or your happiness. When your man is willing to break those walls down listen to him. Find out what your man needs are. They may not be the same needs he had when you got together a year, two years, five or ten years ago.

People change, needs change. Hey may kick, scream and cry when he's stressed. He may communicate his emotions in a different way. Don't be too quick to pass judgment or to be tit for tat and throw back your feelings. If your man is unhappy, do your part to fix it.

Figure out what you can do to help him. When he is happy, it benefits your relationship and benefits your household. At times it takes more from us emotionally, than it takes from the man. There are double standards in relationships. When we accept those standards, it's easier to abide by them.

Yes, the scales may be a little unbalanced, but where you lack, he excels and vice versa. In other words, stop looking at what you feel like you're doing more of and just do what you can offer. If he's not happy, make him happy. It really is that simple.

Now, you could be dealing with a situation that is a little bit different than him saying he's just unhappy in the relationship. For example, you could be dealing with a lack of interest. He may say, he is no longer attracted to you. And that's a whole different conversation and that's why communication (yes, I know I say that a lot!) is extremely important because there's a different route to take if he says he's no longer attracted to you. Woman experience many different factors that contribute to our body's changing. We sacrifice our bodies to bring these men their kids into this world, when a woman is stressed out, that can cause weight gain and hormones, don't even get me started.

For example, I was helping a relationship where a man expressed his dissatisfaction with his fiancé's curvier figure. They had been involved for about six years and after hormonal and emotional changes she gained weight.

Of course, now the woman was insecure and slightly angered being that he was packing some extra pounds as well. Her initial reaction was to express her feelings about his weight. However, I advised her to take a different approach. As with anything, it is not what you say, but how you say it. She first decided for herself that she did want to get healthy and lose weight. Then, per my advice, she signed them both up for a gym membership and convinced him to get healthy and fit with her.

By no means am I telling you, make your man happy at all costs. He should love you for who you are before your appearance. If you have you gained a little weight and you want to lose some pounds, make sure it's for you.

Don't just go and change everything about yourself for a man. Because that's not what this book is all about. You need to be you.

If you acknowledge that you have let yourself, then perhaps work towards getting yourself back.

Even if you never deal with any of those issues you still need to make sure that, not only for him but for yourself, that you keep your marriage spicy; keep it new, keep it exciting. You don't want your relationship to become a chore. Your partner should be your best friend. At the end of the day, he should be able to come to you and laugh about office gossip. If you are into role playing, dress up and surprise him on a weeknight. Don't wait until just Friday, Saturday, or Sunday to do something special and romantic. If that's your normal schedule, switch it up a little bit. Surprise him on a Wednesday. Spend some time together. Make him laugh.

It is necessary to consistently think of new ways to rejuvenate your marriage.

You don't want to be stuck in a fog. I don't want to come home and feel like, "Oh, I gotta deal with this guy again." Switch it up. Cook different meal, plan new activities, buy new lingerie. Keep him guessing.

Ladies you know we love some juicy gossip. Let your man in on some of the juicy gossip. Sometimes I enjoy our conversations a little too much. I've called my husband "Girl" and "Sis" multiple times. He is truly my best friend.

Most importantly, you've got to know what makes this man tick. What gets him going. Your happiness should not be solely dependent on him and the other way around. However, you should receive some happiness just from seeing him happy and from making him happy. It gets boring sitting around doing the same stuff over and over.

So, reinvent your relationship as much as possible. The last thing you want to do is to let your relationship

ever become stagnant. You always want forward movement, positive movement.

We spoil each other in every way possible. My husband has surprised me with the small gifts such as, chocolate covered strawberries to the luxury items such as my truck. It doesn't have to be a holiday; that's known in our house. We don't wait for Christmas or a birthday to spoil each other.

Reinvent your relationship as much as possible. The last thing you want to do is to let your relationship ever become stagnant. You always want forward movement, positive movement. Change and grow with each other, not apart.

CHAPTER SEVEN

A marriage is an ongoing job. The work never stops. These are the best things to do to ensure that you keep your man and your marriage successful.

I've said this before and I'm going to say it again. I'm stressing this because it is the most important aspect of a marriage or in your relationship, and that is communication. As I stated, no relationship just works. You will constantly be pouring into this relationship. Of course, hopefully all positive things, but it is possible to pour in negativity and you have to be very conscious of the energy you pour into your marriage.

Many people confuse communication for just talking. They want to sit down and run off at the mouth. The big part of communication is knowing how to listen. How to shut your mouth and listen to what the other person is saying. I don't mean listening just to respond. Active listening is when you are really hearing what that person has to say so that you can find a solution to the problem.

Don't put a band aid on a bullet wound. Get to the source of these problems. Problems will certainly occur in your relationship. That's inevitable. You are not going to agree on everything and if you cannot talk to each other, I am telling you, your relationship will fail.

The next most important thing you need to have in your marriage is a positive attitude. You'd be surprised how many women enter relationships and marriages with a bad entitled attitude. Sis, technically speaking, no one owes you anything. You deserve the world you are not owed it.

Every situation in your marriage should be handled with a positive attitude. You will get angry sometime but that does not justify being negative. A negative mind cannot think positive thoughts.

Often women treat their bosses at work with more positivity and respect than they do their own man. If your boss upsets you at work know, in order to keep your job, that you must bite your tongue and deal with it. When your mom pisses you off, you respectfully agree to disagree. Oh, but let your man do something. You have no problem unleashing the inner bitch on him.

I realize that it's very hard to stop and check yourself. To humble and put yourself back in your place. Nonetheless, your man deserves to be handled with positivity and the upmost respect.

Of course, that goes for both sides. The energy you put into your marriage is exactly what you're going to get out of it. Don't blame him if he's coming home every day with an attitude when you meet him and greet him with the exact same attitude.

Pause the judgement and think about all the things that you could do better. Perhaps your shortcomings will humble you and force you to deal with the situation with a better attitude.

The bottom line is, your attitude is very critical in a relationship. Don't go out in this world and tiptoe around others, then come home and take it all out on your man.

ARAINE ROBINSON

Never underestimate the importance of your attitude and the power of your words.

Once you have your attitude in check, the third most important thing to do in your marriage or relationship is to always be willing to compromise. Sometimes you do have to be selfless. While at other times you will need to meet him in the middle. Understand the magnitude of your actions. Honestly, about 80% of the success of the relationship is dependent on us.

There are always going to be times in your relationship where one of you is working harder than the other. Of course, there are times where you must understand that your efforts may not always be immediately reciprocated.

For example, my husband owns a very busy business and it is extremely taxing on him.

Once he got more agents and business increased, I noticed he was coming home irritable. Now, like most men, my husband is not a super emotional guy. He will not cry on my shoulder. Being an attentive, compromising wife I compromise my wants to ensure that my husband is taken care of. Even if it's something as simple as putting the kids to bed a little bit earlier and not expecting them to help so much. When I know he is really stressed I will have a hot bath ready for him after dinner.

Those little small compromises go a long way. There could be times where it could be a positive thing. He gets a big promotion at work; be there for him, be excited for him. Be his number one fan, his cheerleader.

Now, let me speak on this as I skipped over this issue. I've touched on a man cheating, but I haven't touched on the opposite side. Let me just say this, ladies. Once again, there are double Is it okay? No, but is it expected? Yes. We understand that it is a possibility that a man will cheat. We understand that their eyes wander, but don't get it confused that as a woman, that's not expected. When men cheat, it is usually just for sexual purposes; it is not always for a long drawn out reason. When women cheat, the reason is often for emotional reasons.

Two wrongs don't make a right. If you cheat out of retaliation, you're doing damage to yourself. I speak a lot on how to approach a man's mistakes but understand that if you decide to cheat on your husband, boyfriend or fiancé, you're hurting yourself.

If your man does something that you don't appreciate, handle that issue with whatever consequences you see fit. But to stay and take his infidelity as a hall pass speaks on who you are as a woman. I'm going to be honest, even if he takes you back, he will never look at you the same. That man will never respect you. We live in times where most people don't practice celibacy prior to marriage. Going into the relationship, you know generally that this is not your partner's only sexual experience and that's fine. But once that relationship is established the only person that should have the honor of even looking at your body is the man you are committed to.

As women it is up to us to value our bodies. Society tells us sex sells and being promiscuous is a form of expression. We've got to reel that in and understand, like I said, we are goddesses.

Not every man deserves to see your body, to touch your body, to be inside your body. What a man does should not dictate your reaction. Let him be wrong all by himself. If you pour your best into your union regardless of his actions, if things go wrong then you will know without a doubt that you it was at no fault of your own.

The day my husband (then boyfriend) proposed to me is one of the best days of my life. Although I was confident that he was the man for me, I was also confident that I was not ready to be a wife. I was not mature enough to agree to disagree, I still wanted to prove my point and be right. I was not mentally prepared to give all that I felt was required of a wife, I was still selfish. We were engaged for two years before I reached a point when it just clicked. When I had to boss up or punk down. I wanted a happy healthy marriage with my man, and I was ready to stop preventing myself from leveling up.

I changed my mindset and the way I approached my husband. It was no longer about being right or winning an argument.

effectively communicating and resolving any issues we face were my goals and to this day that is how I operate in marriage. If my husband is in his feelings and being petty, I don't get on his level, I work through it. And if he decides at any time that he wants to act a fool, that's on him. My vows are for me to honor and that's what I do.

And on top of that I know that I am an amazing woman all the way around. Every woman should appreciate and love herself, flaws and all. With that being said, a random man should not have the honor of having you, if even for one night.

CHAPTER EIGHT

Things will change throughout the years of your relationship. In the early part faze, especially if you're young, you may want to go out clubbing together. Go on dates frequently outside of the house and it hit every concert that comes to town. However, for most people, as they get older, wisdom comes in and things change. You may find that now you prefer a dinner and a movie at home. How you start is not how you finish. The key is to be very vocal. And to evolve with your partner throughout the entire relationship.

A lot of things change in relationships. Not only how you date and where you date, but things such as chemistry and intimacy.

In relationships and in life one thing that is certain is change, and if you don't prepare yourself for that and vocalize what's going on, then you're going to have a lot of problems in your relationship. If you have remained the same person year after year, then there's a strong possibility that you need therapy.

I once worked with a young man who was at a crossroad in his relationship. He had been with his fiancé' for 3 years and had just had their first child. In the early stages of their relationship they both enjoyed going to parties, drinking and frankly being irresponsible. Once their baby was born, he longer enjoyed partying and getting wasted.

While he worked to create a stable environment for his family, they began to have serious issues in the relationship. He assumed she would mature, settle down and live a more responsible life.

The problem began we he assumed. It was back to scheduled programming as soon as she had their baby. She was back to the partying and drinking and wanted her partner in crime to join her. First and Foremost, once they decided to be together, they should've expressed their expectations for the relationship. However, they did not so he had no idea that she didn't have the values he had.

They did not have effective communication so the anger would just fester until one of them exploded. If they had communicated frequently, she would've been aware of his changes and he would have known she wanted things to stay the same.

Be proactive instead of reactive. Don't just wing it. Naturally everything will not go according to plan, but enough will. Therefore, you will be prepared for the unexpected times.

A helpful tip is to pick one day every month that you designate to having a deep conversation. That will be the time when you both discuss any issues. As well as the time to compliment and critique your partner. Ask your man what he wants and needs in the relationship. It is easier to avoid conversations to prevent arguments, but relationships aren't easy.

During your talks with your man be certain to encourage him. Men work well with positive reinforcement. No one wants to be picked apart on a daily basis. Criticism will make anyone shut down. Men need our confirmation. Habitually praise him. That reassurance that you appreciate his effort encourages him to continue pleasing you. It can be hard for us when we feel overworked and underappreciated. However, give what you'd like to receive. Set the tone.

Most relationships experience issues due to the lack of security. If you don't feel secure in the fact that your man will listen to you then you will be hesitant to open up to him. The same goes for your man. You will probably be surprised how much you can get your man to open up when you make him feel secure and confident in doing so. Let that man express himself.

For the most part, whatever your man is asking you to do, it should pretty much align with who you are and how you two set up your relationship. It shouldn't be too outrageous demands of what you're asking and what he's asking. By no means am I ever telling you to lose yourself for this man. And if he asks you something that you're not comfortable with, that goes against your morals; don't do it. But this late in your relationship you should both be on the same page. Make sure that you both feel as if you can express yourself.

Now with that being said, you know what he likes, you know what he wants and vice versa. You still need to find a way to be spontaneous. You don't want the relationship to get boring.

Clearly life does not always go according to plan. When it comes to having a good time with your partner, there is no specific time for that. When the time presents itself, have some unplanned fun. If you are taking a bath invite him to join you If he is washing the car, go "accidently" spray him with the water. Have a little fun. Remind him and yourself why you got together.

Nobody wants a stale relationship. You should always work on your relationship, but your relationship shouldn't feel like a job. If there are no kids involved or they visit grandmas for the weekends, take a quick road trip or get a hotel room for a night. You can be in the beginning stages or near your last days with this man. Your relationship will require constant work, so make sure that you make this journey fun as well.

CHAPTER NINE

You might have heard the phrase, a couple that prays together, stays together. This is a very true statement. I don't think it's mandatory to pray with each other every time you pray. However, you will both have to pray to God to keep your marriage, engagement and/or relationship strong. You both will have the world's negative energy trying to pull you apart. What will keep you grounded and together is God. Make sure that both of you are praying every day to keep the negatives of the world away from your commitment to one another.

In addition to praying with each other you need to pray for each other. Every time your man leaves the house, the pressure of the world is on his shoulders. We expect him to provide and protect. There are billions of people in this world. That man is literally in competition with every other man around him. This is not a race or a cultural thing. This is a man and woman thing I'm talking about. When that man goes into this world, no matter what his profession is, there are hundreds, thousands, millions of other men fighting for the highest position in that field. With all that stress packed onto an overflowing plate of feelings, needs, temptations and other issues; he needs as much prayer as he can receive. Pray for his overall health, both mental and physical.

There is power in prayer. When you're praying with each other and for each other it helps shield your relationship from the evils that can destroy your marriage.

Hopefully, before you even entered your relationship, you had a good relationship with God. Which means you probably prayed for many things in your life. Perhaps you prayed for a good man to spend the rest of your life with. And if your prayer were answered and you got your man, then don't stop praying now.

Marriage, legally speaking, is just the government acknowledging you two as one. There are some states that recognize a "common law marriage" after seven years where you don't have to ever make a commitment before God.

However, once you enter a holy union or a marriage, you are making a promise to God. If you felt inclined to make that commitment before God, then you need to be certain to keep God in your marriage.

There are times in a relationship where you are going to be tried. When either of you go out into this world, single married, engaged, whatever, you are facing a lot of negativities in different forms. If you believe in good, you must believe in the bad. Therefore, you should be praying frequently. Pray for that promotion, pray for your health, pray for your union.

Keep in mind that only God can judge you. Often people care more about the opinions of their friends and families before their obligations to God. I've dealt with a lot of relationships where the family feel the need to overly express their opinions and views on a relationship. My advice is Pray on it and do what's best for you. If God is in your relationship and your heart is in it and you've carefully outweighed all the pro's and con's, no other opinions should be considered.

Consider your source when seeking advice. If your parents have been married 40 plus years and they have a successful marriage, you're damn right you should take some advice from them. They have been through it and had success. But your best friend with two baby daddies and multiple failed relationships should not be counselling you.

Rely on your faith and the bond with God to get you through your marriage. If you have prayed on something and you still want to consult with close family, or a best friend then do so. But keep in mind a chef cannot give a doctor advice. That doesn't discredit the chef. He may be one hell of a chef in the kitchen, but he or she is cannot diagnosis you. When prayer is frequent, and your faith is strong your marriage will match that strength.

CHAPTER TEN

Now, what I'm going to say just might be the most important part to this book. So, listen carefully ladies. Before you go taking this expert advice and applying it to your life, you need to make sure that you are even ready to be in a fully committed relationship. Ask yourself, are you mentally, physically, and emotionally ready to be at any level of a relationship? A lot of women carry over baggage and scars from abusive, toxic, and unhealthy previous relationships. Before you jump into another relationship, you need to take time to heal so that you can be your best you for a new man.

We probably wouldn't have so many failed relationships and marriages if we took the time to really understand who we were as women and to really become whole before we jumped into a relationship. As I stated, a lot of us have baggage that we don't even recognize. We start our relationship with a lifetime of baggage. Never realizing that we gravitate towards that same toxicity that we claim to not want.

Peeling back the layers of buried issues is one of the hardest things to do. It is hard to be real with yourself and accept responsibility that you may be the reason for your own hardships. Stop and ask yourself why you keep attracting the same kind of guys, why you have a history of failed relationships, why your love life is lacking love. Keep it real with yourself.

There are so many traumatized women that don't see how they are still being affected and don't know how to heal. Yet they are out here claiming to be "wife material". A damaged young lady becomes a damaged grown woman. Young girls need to be taught how to care for themselves mentally and emotionally prior to dating. Without that knowledge she will not be prepared for a relationship and will likely endure heart break.

As for the women who have experienced failed relationships, make that fail into a lesson. It is much easier to blame others rather than accept fault. You need to figure out exactly what it is about you that goes against what you are trying to achieve.

111

It is not uncommon to grow up in a household with no real example of true love or healthy relationships. Therefore, when you get into relationships, you don't know how to act. Even while attempting to "break the cycle", it is possible to still display toxic traits.

Before you apply anything that I've said answer these questions. How long have you been single? Is there any trauma you need to heal from? Have I taken enough time to work on me? What do I really have to offer a man in my current state? Can I be a better me? Dig deep and work on yourself. Don't set yourself up for failure by getting yourself into something you are not ready for.

When you are silently dealing with unresolved issues you may find that you are easily angered. Nobody has the power to make you act out of character. Your actions are a direct reflection of your character. You just learned how to suppress it and in a successful relationship there is no for a ticking time bomb attitude.

You never know when your true love is going to walk into your life, but you need to be prepared for when he does come.

When you are truly healed, and the baggage has been dumped it will be so rewarding when you find your man. At that point, you will in a better head space. You will be acting from love, rather than hurt. You will know how to respond to different situations in a calm, mild manner. You will be accepting of constructive criticism, just as you would a compliment. You be willing to pour everything you have into your relationship because you don't fear being let down, as you were in the past. You will face obstacles in your life and relationship with a clear level mind and heart.

Let me be the first to tell you, married life is amazing. Knowing that you have a man that will be by your side no matter what is priceless. Knowing that I am on this roller coaster of life with my best friend makes all the difficulties of marriage worth it all.

ARIANE ROBINSON

If nobody else on this planet has your best interest at heart, your husband does. It's a beautiful thing to know you are cherished, that he would do anything to ensure your happiness and wellbeing. To know that your husband just happens to be you're your soul mate and best friend, is truly an amazing feeling.

If you are a woman who's looking for that, don't stop. Your man is out there. The good outweighs the bad and is worth every obstacle you have faced and stand to face. So, go find you a man girl and keep him!

CPSIA information can be obtained
at www.ICGtesting.com
Printed in the USA
FFHW012336061119
56000316-61849FF

9 780578 592640